West Country
WOODLAND WALKS

Acknowledgements

Text: Forest Enterprise
Photography: Forest Life Picture Library, Rod Leslie,
                             Robin Khan, Philip Chambers, Dave Pedlar,
                             Tamara Loakes, Stan Abbot, Alan Eves
Illustrations: Design and Interpretation Branch,
                             Forest Enterprise
Editors: Donald Greig, Tracy Hunt
Designers: Brian Skinner, Don Friston
Mapping: Jim Newman

The tree illustrations on pp.58-61 are taken from the leaflet 'Easy Guide to Forest Trees and their Uses', produced for Forest Enterprise North and East England Region by Phrogg Design and available from Forest Shops.

The publishers would like to thank Chris Probert and Forest Enterprise for their assistance and co-operation in the compilation of this guide.

© Jarrold Publishing and Ordnance Survey 1996
Maps © Crown copyright 1996

Jarrold Publishing   ISBN 0-7117-0857-6
Ordnance Survey   ISBN 0-3190-0861-4

While every care has been taken to ensure the accuracy of the route directions, the publishers cannot accept responsibility for errors or omissions, or for changes in details given. The forests are not static, and due to forestry work and maintenance some re-routing may be necessary from time to time. Also, paths that are easy and pleasant for walking in fine conditions may become slippery, muddy and difficult in wet weather, while stepping stones across rivers and streams may become impassable.

If you find an inaccuracy in either the text or maps, please write to Jarrold Publishing or Ordnance Survey respectively at one of the addresses below.
First published 1996 by Jarrold Publishing and Ordnance Survey

Jarrold Publishing, Whitefriars, Norwich NR3 1TR
Ordnance Survey, Romsey Road, Southampton SO16 4GU

Printed in Great Britain by Jarrold Printing, Norwich 1/96

Contents

Keymap	4
At-a-Glance… chart and map key	6
Introduction	8

Dorset

Walk 1	Moors Valley	18
Walk 2	Ramsdown	20
Walk 3	Wareham	22
Walk 4	Affpuddle	24

Somerset

Walk 5	Neroche	26
Walk 6	Quantock	28

Devon

Walk 7	Ashclyst	30
Walk 8	Stoke Woods	32
Walk 9	Eggesford – Taw Valley	34
Walk 10	Eggesford – Heywood	36
Walk 11	Abbeyford Wood	38
Walk 12	Haldon – Long Walk	40
Walk 13	Haldon – Mamhead All Abilities	42
Walk 14	Haldon – Butterfly Walk	44
Walk 15	Bellever	46
Walk 16	Fernworthy	48
Walk 17	Denham	50
Walk 18	Cann Wood	52

Cornwall

Walk 19	Deerpark Woods	54
Walk 20	Cardinham Woods	56

Guide to common trees	58
Useful Information	63
Index	64

WOODLAND WALKS

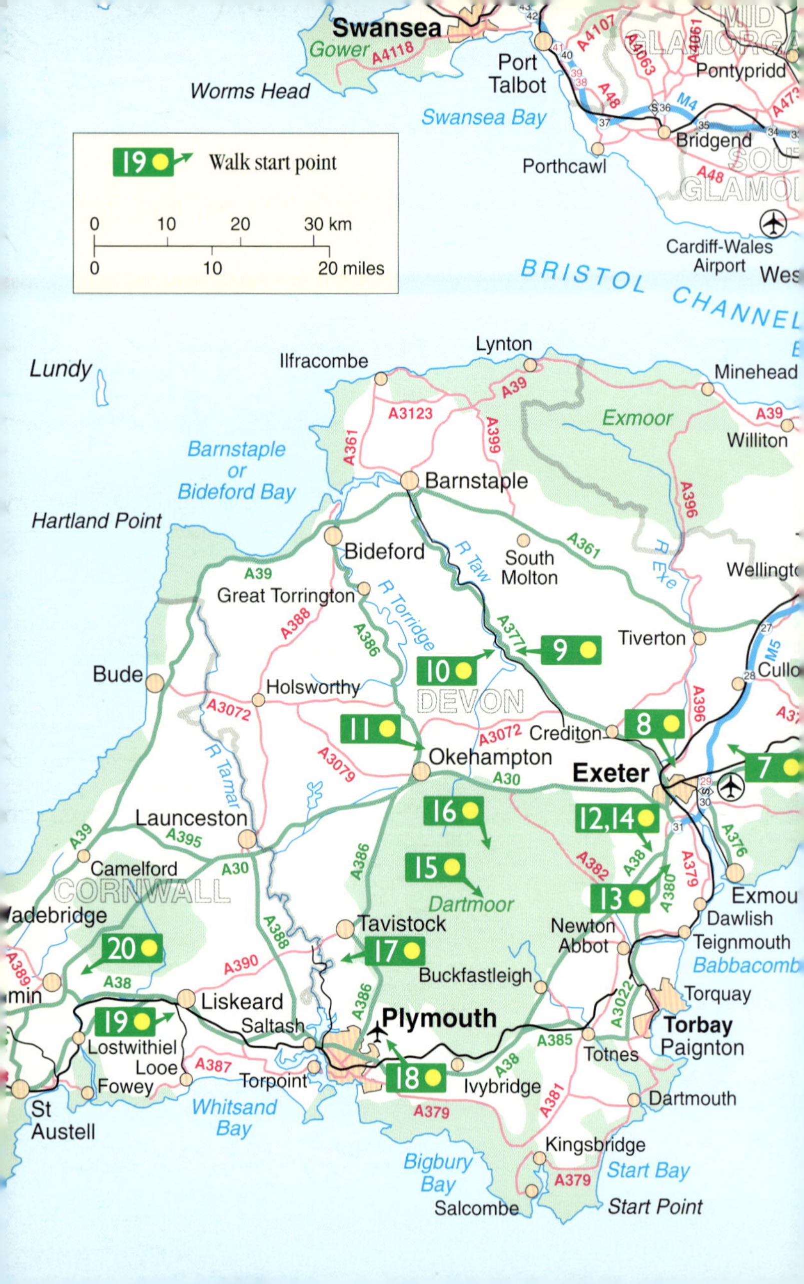

Walk start point
0 10 20 30 km
0 10 20 miles
Swansea
Gower
Worms Head
Port Talbot
Swansea Bay
Pontypridd
Bridgend
Porthcawl
Cardiff-Wales Airport
BRISTOL CHANNEL
Lundy
Ilfracombe
Lynton
Minehead
Exmoor
Williton
Barnstaple or Bideford Bay
Barnstaple
Hartland Point
Bideford
South Molton
Wellington
Great Torrington
R Taw
R Torridge
R Exe
Tiverton
Bude
Holsworthy
DEVON
Crediton
Okehampton
Exeter
R Tamar
Launceston
Camelford
CORNWALL
Wadebridge
Dartmoor
Tavistock
Newton Abbot
Exmouth
Dawlish
Teignmouth
Babbacombe
Buckfastleigh
Torquay
Liskeard
Saltash
Plymouth
Torbay
Paignton
Lostwithiel
Looe
Fowey
Torpoint
Totnes
Ivybridge
Dartmouth
St Austell
Whitsand Bay
Bigbury Bay
Kingsbridge
Start Bay
Salcombe
Start Point
1 7 8 9 10 11 12,14 13 15 16 17 18 19 20

Chepstow
Newport
CARDIFF
Avonmouth
Clevedon
Penarth
Bristol
Bath
AVON
Tetbury
Swindon
Malmesbury
R Avon
Yate
M4
M5
M32
Chippenham
Calne
Marlborough
Devizes
Trowbridge
WILTSHIRE
Westbury
Warminster
Amesbury
Frome
Cheddar
Mendip Hills
Wells
Glastonbury
Shepton Mallet
Street
SOMERSET
Mere
Wilton
Salisbury
Wincanton
Langport
Ilchester
Shaftesbury
Cranborne Chase & West Wiltshire Downs
New Forest
R Avon
Ilminster
Yeovil
Sherborne
Fordingbridge
Crewkerne
DORSET
Chard
Blandford Forum
Wimborne Minster
Ringwood
Honiton
Axminster
Christchurch
Bridport
Dorchester
Poole
Bournemouth
Seaton
Lyme Regis
Wareham
Poole Bay
Isle of Purbeck
Swanage
Lyme Bay
Weymouth
Fortuneswell
St Aldhelm's or St Alban's Head
Bill of Portland
ENGLISH CHANNEL

At-a

	Forest Walk	Grade	Time	Length	Car Park	Picnic Site	Toile
1	**Moors Valley**	△	50 mins	1½m	✔	✔	✔
2	**Ramsdown**	▲	40 mins	1½m	✔	✔	✘
3	**Wareham**	△	2 hrs	3½m	✔	✔	✘
4	**Affpuddle**	▲	1 hr	1¾m	✔	✔	✘
5	**Neroche**	▲	45 mins	1½m	✔	✔	✘
6	**Quantock**	▲	1¼ hrs	2¼m	✔	✔	✔
7	**Ashclyst**	▲	1¼ hrs	2½m	✔	✔	✘
8	**Stoke Woods**	▲	45 mins	1½m	✔	✔	✘
9	**Eggesford – Taw**	△	40 mins	0.8m	✔	✔	✔
10	**Eggesford – Hey.**	▲	2 hrs	2½m	✔	✘	✘
11	**Abbeyford**	△	1½ hrs	2m	✔	✔	✘
12	**Haldon – Long**	▲	4 hrs	8¾m	✔	✔	✘
13	**Haldon – M'head**	△	30 mins	1m	✔	✔	✘
14	**Haldon – B'fly**	▲	1½ hrs	2¼m	✔	✔	✘
15	**Bellever**	▲	1½ hrs	3m	✔	✔	✔
16	**Fernworthy**	▲	1¼ hrs	2½m	✔	✔	✔
17	**Denham**	▲	1 hr	2½m	✔	✘	✘
18	**Cann Wood**	△	1½ hrs	2¾m	✔	✘	✘
19	**Deerpark Woods**	▲	2 hrs	3½m	✔	✔	✘
20	**Cardinham**	▲	2 hrs	3½m	✔	✔	✔

Cycling and Horse Riding are available in the designated woods, but not on the trails featured

WEST COUNTRY

ance…

More Walks	Wildlife Interest	Historic Interest	Water Interest	Cycling	Horse Riding*
✔	✔	✘	✘	✔	✔
✘	✔	✔	✘	✘	✔
✔	✔	✔	✔	✔	✔
✘	✔	✔	✔	✔	✔
✔	✔	✔	✘	✘	✘
✘	✔	✘	✔	✔	✔
✔	✔	✘	✘	✘	✔
✔	✔	✘	✘	✘	✘
✔	✔	✔	✘	✔	✘
✘	✔	✔	✘	✔	✘
✘	✔	✘	✘	✔	✘
✔	✔	✔	✔	✘	✔
✔	✔	✔	✘	✘	✘
✔	✔	✘	✘	✘	✔
✔	✔	✔	✔	✔	✘
✔	✔	✔	✔	✔	✘
✘	✔	✘	✔	✘	✔
✔	✔	✔	✘	✔	✔
✘	✔	✘	✘	✘	✘
✔	✔	✔	✔	✔	✘

*By permit from Forest District Offices (see p.63)

KEY TO MAP SYMBOLS

- **P** Parking
- **i** Information
- **WC** Toilets
- Picnic Site
- **1** Point of Interest
- Coniferous
- Non Coniferous

- Easy-going
- Moderate-going
- Demanding
- Sensible footwear
- Waterproof footwear
- Hillwalking boots

WOODLAND WALKS

Introduction

Welcome to the West's woods!

The walks in this guide are a great introduction to the beautiful scenery of this popular holiday area. From bleak Dartmoor tors to cosy Cornish valleys, each walk has been carefully planned by local foresters. You'll find the best views, the beauty of the trees, countryside and wildlife, and history as well. All the walks except one are an easy half day expedition and waymarked by colour coded posts, so you don't have to be an expert map reader.

The fruit of the Corsican pine – see pages 58–61 for details of other common species.

Walks start from Forestry Commission car parks (Fernworthy starts from the South West Water car park) and each one includes directions on how to get there. The start is easy to find, so just check the colour of the posts you have to follow as sometimes several walks

An inviting oakwood forest scene.

start from one place. Follow the path until you see posts marking a corner, and eventually you'll be led back to your car. You won't need special equipment for these walks: a pair of stout shoes with commando-type soles or trainers will be fine except in wet winter weather when some paths can get muddy.

Each walk is different, so check the description before you start. The path at Mamhead in Haldon Forest, for instance, is built for wheelchairs and is ideal for anyone who has to use a stick or take a pushchair. It leads to a spectacular view of the Exe estuary. The Sika Trail in Wareham Forest and the trail at Cann Wood are both on flat ground, but Bellever, the Quantocks and the Silvermine Trail at Cardinham are hilly.

The walks follow forest roads, tracks and paths through the trees. There are bridges over streams and gates or stiles in fences, and no barbed wire or impenetrable thickets! Occasionally, parts of a walk may be closed for timber harvesting, but there will be a clearly marked diversion to follow. Best of all, there is freedom to roam in all these woods, meaning you can wander wherever you like and don't have to stick to the waymarked route. These are very much your woods, nationally owned and dedicated to multi-purpose management for timber, recreation, conservation and heritage.

Glossy leaves of a Sweet Chestnut in flower.

Forest History

The woods all have a story to tell. Over the centuries they've seen some of the earliest peoples to live in Britain, wars, industry and, in our own century, the new woodlands of the Forestry Commission. In the beginning our distant ancestors hacked clearings from forest covering the whole of England. They found the poorest soils, where the forest was thinnest – high or dry land, like Dartmoor or the sandy soils of Dorset. The evidence of their civilisations remains to this day and includes standing stones, stone circles and rows, and remains of hundreds of huts that cover Dartmoor and Bronze Age burial barrows in Dorset. Later, high points were chosen for medieval castles at Heywood and Castle Neroche, while the silver mine at Cardinham is a reminder of the south west's booming mining industries of the last century.

Our woods feel marvellously natural, but they have been shaped by people's needs over many centuries. Once, medieval people used oak and hazel coppices for firewood and building. Later, as industrialisation developed, the woods were cut for charcoal and oak bark for tanning. They were not destroyed: native trees like oak grow again from the cut stump and as long as woods were useful to people they were protected. But charcoal was replaced by coke and gradually many woods fell into disuse as the old rural industries declined and there was little use for woodland products.

Mature Scots Pines reach for the sky.

The Forestry Commission

The U-boat campaign of World War I transformed British forestry: never again must Britain be dependant on imports to keep the coal mines going. The Forestry Commission was set up in 1919, taking over existing woodlands including Cardinham, Ashclyst and the Quantocks and planting open country like the Sika Trail, Bellever, Haldon and Mamhead. The very first trees were planted in Flashdown Wood at Eggesford, where they are commemorated by a memorial plaque. Another plaque near the main Eggesford forest car park commemorates a tree planted by Her Majesty the Queen.

The Forestry Commission introduced conifers because they grow faster than our native broadleaves, make good, straight pit props and grow well on poor soils. From small beginnings the national forests now cover more than 2½ million acres (1 million ha), from Cornwall to Kent and up to the north of Scotland. Since 1992 Forest Enterprise, the land management arm of the Forestry Commission, has looked after these forests.

Know your Trees

It is the forester's skill to match the right trees to the very different environments which you'll find along the walks in this book. Look out for the different trees – it's not difficult to identify the main species. Pines always do best on the driest soils, especially along the Haldon and Sika Trail walks, where there are mainly Scots pine and Corsican pine. Spruce, Norway spruce from Europe and Sitka from America like the wet ground of Dartmoor. Soft needled Douglas fir grow huge on the best valley slope soils of Quantock, Eggesford and Cardinham, along with pale green larch, one of the only conifers to lose its needles in winter. You'll find the greatest concentration of broadleaved trees in the oldest forests and on the richer soils. Oak is one of the commonest, often with hazel underneath the big trees. Ash and beech are both common also, with alder along streams and birch the commonest broadleaf at Haldon and in the woodlands featured in Dorset.

For a pictorial round-up of some of the commonest trees, see the illustrations on pp.58–62.

Forestry at Work

On all these walks you can see forestry at work. Choosing the right tree is only the beginning. Search amongst the branches for new young trees on open ground where mature trees have been felled – the start of a new, renewable forest. Sometimes the ground may have been cultivated to improve the young tree's growth. These small trees have come from a Forest Enterprise nursery and are two to three years old when they are planted out. For the first five years they must be protected against weeds and grazing animals such as deer or rabbits.

The growing trees close ranks, into a dense, dark teenage thicket, which some say is the least attractive stage in the forest's life. Thinning then starts to open the forest up – look for where rows have been removed to allow workers and tractors in to farm small trees for fencing posts or rustic garden furniture. From now on the trees will be thinned every five years, with the fewer and fewer remaining trees getting bigger and bigger until they are eventually felled at commercial maturity at 50-60 years old. Then their valuable wood will go for saw timber, to build houses or farm buildings.

Although the distant buzz of a chainsaw may be your only contact with foresters working in the woods, forestry plays an important and varied part in the rural scene today. As well as workers felling trees, there are foresters who plan and supervise forest management, craftsmen who plant and weed the young trees, and wildlife rangers who protect them from damage by deer, rabbits and grey squirrels. Civil engineers maintain the network of roads and lorry drivers haul timber to the factory, while recreation rangers look after walks and car parks, meet visitors and lead school parties and special events.

Conservation

Once our forests were managed just for timber but now Forest Enterprise has a much bigger job to do. Today our national forests are valued for their beauty, as a place to walk and for their

A Forestry Commission machine operator using a grapple-head harvester to process a stand of Sitka Spruce.

Woodland adventures are suitable for all ages.

wildlife and history. Each forest has a design plan for its future, improving on the original Forestry Commission planting. Felling areas are sculpted to the landscape and the age of felling adjusted for a more varied and interesting forest. A dramatic ridge like Haldon takes special care to avoid ugly notches in the skyline. Edges along roads are landscaped for the walker's interest and for wildlife. The beautiful streamsides at Cardinham and Deerpark have been carefully thinned. Special habitats, including broadleaved trees, streamsides and clearings are carefully managed and trees are removed from ancient sites like tumuli or burial mounds to help preserve them.

In addition, a number of places have been designated as Sites of Special Scientific Interest (SSSI). These are areas of land of special nature conservation value, including geological or physiographic interest. The designation applies throughout Great Britain and sites in England are notified by English Nature.

Other places have been designated as Areas of Outstanding Natural Beauty (AONB), a description which applies to a wide range of nationally significant and traditional landscapes. It is in everyone's interests to look after these areas in terms of development and land management. Such areas are designated in England by the Countryside Commission.

Forest Fauna and Birdlife

The Sika Trail at Wareham Forest was planted on lowland heath, which is today an internationally rare habitat, home to endangered species like sand lizard and Dartford warbler. As you walk the trail you'll see how the forest has been cut back to allow heather to grow again. Sand lizard aren't easy to see, but you might be lucky with the

WOODLAND WALKS

The Tawny owl is perfectly at home in the oak forests.

big Sika deer the trail is named after. Come here for a summer evening walk or visit Haldon to hear the mechanical churring song of nightjar. Although the freshly felled forest looks a messy battlefield to us, this is where nightjar nest on the ground, their mottled plumage acting as daytime camouflage from prowling predators.

Each age of the forest is home to different wildlife – conifers don t cone every year, but when they do the forest rings to the chipping calls of crossbill flocks high among the biggest trees. Birds of prey need the big trees for nesting, too. The commonest are buzzard and sparrowhawk – the former circling lazily over every south-west wood, the latter dashing amongst the trees on rounded wings to pounce on small birds. Birdwatchers flock to Haldon for its rare Honey buzzards, best seen from the special viewpoint just down the road from the main car park. Once extinct in Britain, goshawk now hunt these forests again. Similar to sparrowhawk but bigger, they are secretive and hard to see.

Butterflies luxuriate in clearings and glades. Silver-washed Fritillaries power fly the rides of Ashclyst, Neroche and Haldon. Look for White

Admirals in the big oaks at Ashclyst. In 15 years of careful management the Powerline reserve at Haldon has been transformed from mown grass to a mosaic of meadow and scrub habitats, home to over 30 species of butterfly including Wood White and Pearl-bordered Fritillary. Glades are where the deer feed, too. Red deer, our largest land mammal, are a speciality of the Quantocks – be very quiet if you want to see them before they see you. Not so wild are the wily ponies that find their way through fences from the commons of the Quantocks.

You can be your own nature detective on these walks. Watch for wildlife signs – the imprint of deer crossing a muddy track, or for hazel nut shells gnawed by dormice – signs of these tiny nocturnal creatures, rarely seen. North Devon is 'Tarka country'. After years when farm pollution poisoned Tarka's home rivers, otters are now back again and you might be lucky to see a spraint – their droppings – near the river Taw at Eggesford.

Walks and More

There's exotic wildlife at Moors Valley as well – an extraordinary playtrail of snakes, spiders, crocodiles and loggosaurs, all sculpted from wood produced in the surrounding forest. You won't be able to drag children away from it. With a visitor centre, shop and cafe this is one of the sites with a few more facilities. Another is Cardinham in Cornwall, with its woodland café, cycle hire and adventure trail for children. As well as walking, there's cycling, wildlife watching and other activities in many of our forests. If you want to find out more, why not join one of the regular events run by Forest Enterprise recreation rangers – everything from teddy bear's picnics to dusk Nightjar watches!

We hope you enjoy walking in your woods. They are a living landscape, peaceful yet productive – of wildlife as well as timber. They are truly sustainable, since new young trees quickly replace those which have been felled and each part of the forest is home to different animals and plants. Our aim at Forest Enterprise is to make them even better by imaginative management – and as foresters we must look far into the future, trying to provide today for the needs of people and the environment 50 or even 100 years into the future.

Forest Code

Visit your forests and help us to protect them. We want you to enjoy the forest experience and Forest Enterprise welcomes you. Please let others enjoy the same pleasures, so when you visit a forest or a woodland managed by Forest Enterprise, please remember the Forest Code (see p.16).

WOODLAND WALKS

Remember the Forest Code

- Take home only your litter and memories
- Respect the peace and quiet of the forest and its wildlife
- Keep clear of all tree felling and other operations
- Never light fires and, smokers – **Take Care!**
- Cycle with care
- Dogs are welcome. Please keep them under control and **never** let them foul paths or visitor areas
- Cars and motor bikes are only allowed on Forest Drives
- Camping and caravanning are encouraged, but **only** on our campsites
- Permits are required for horse riding, fishing and shooting

A note on safety and security…

Because of the shelter provided by the trees, the forests never get as cold as it does in the open, but nevertheless remember the British climate and take a light waterproof if there's any chance of inclement weather. In addition, since all the walks start at car parks, we recommend that you don't leave anything valuable in your car, especially not a handbag, and that you hide empty binocular or camera cases.

How to Use this Guide

The chart on pages 6 and 7 shows more information about the walks featured in this guide, including which forests offer additional attractions such as extra walks, horse riding and cycling on waymarked routes. By using the chart you can select the walks which suit you best.

For instance, if you want to go to a wood which has toilets and a children's play area, the chart will show you that Moors Valley and Cardinham are good options. Alternatively, if you want to go for a longer, more demanding walk, why not try the Heywood Trail at Eggesford or Deerpark?

The chart also indicates our grade for each trail. 'Easy-going' means you will not encounter steep slopes here; 'Moderate-going' is for walks which require a bit more effort; while 'Demanding' routes are exactly what they say they are.

Finally, please note that certain abbreviations are used throughout the descriptions for the walks: '**FC**' stands for Forestry Commission (eg: 'FC car park'); **SSSI** denotes a Site of Special Scientific Interest; and **AONB** signifies an Area of Outstanding Natural Beauty.

Happy Walking!

WOODLAND WALKS

Moors Valley Forest

LOOKOUT WALK

Grade	⚠
Distance	1½ miles (2.4km)
Timing	50 mins
Footwear	👢
Waymarker	Follow green waymarker
Parking	Moors Valley Country Park and Forest car park – pay and display.

Start point The entrance to the car park is off the Horton road in Ashley Heath, equidistant between the Ashley Heath roundabout and Three Legged Cross. Look for the first waymarker 200ft (60m) outside the Visitor Centre, then proceed along a wide gravel track.

The Lookout provides a particularly good vantage point for visitors to the forest.

Moors Valley Forest was formerly known as Ashley Heath and was bought by the Forestry Commission in 1920 from the Normanton family (Somerley Estate). It forms the lower third of Ringwood Forest and is managed jointly along with the Country Park by Forest Enterprise and East Dorset District Council. As well as offering an attractive walk, the forest also has a playtrail which will keep children of all ages amused. The route takes you through quieter parts of the forest.

The first section is flat with views overlooking the adjacent golf course which is part of the country park. You soon approach a junction where you will have the option of a clockwise or anti-clockwise walk.

Take the anti-clockwise route and continue through pines in various stages of growth. The heather provides a purple

WALK 1

tinge in the summer and thrives where the trees are still young. The trees here are predominantly Scots and Corsican pine (**1**). The path winds its way through tall, red-trunked Scots pines and then over a footbridge. Standing in the crossroads where the wide bridleway bisects the trail, you will notice a fenced fire pond (**2**) 330ft (100m) to the right, which supports gauze-winged dragonflies in the summer. The blue-green needled tree at one side is a Sitka spruce, an unusual tree to be found on this site since it generally prefers deeper, moist peaty soil. Its single needles are sharp and stiff.

The trail follows a gentle incline up a hill covered with young Corsican pines to the Lookout (**3**) from which the walk takes its name. This gives shelter from rain and sun, together with views south over the country park and visitor centre to Hurn Forest and Poole Basin. Tower Park and the Purbeck Hills can be seen in the distance to the south west. The different type and age of trees in many shades of green gives the forest a collage-like appearance at this point.

Descending from the Lookout, keep an eye open for one of four ancient Bronze Age burial mounds on the skyline to the right, now permanently cleared of trees. Also watch out for reptiles such as the adder which occasionally basks on the warm south-facing slopes of the hill. You may also see roe deer, Little owls, sparrowhawks and kestrels, all of which hunt in this area, together with the Dartford warbler.

The route turns south back towards the golf course, crosses the bridleway again and runs down to the car park.

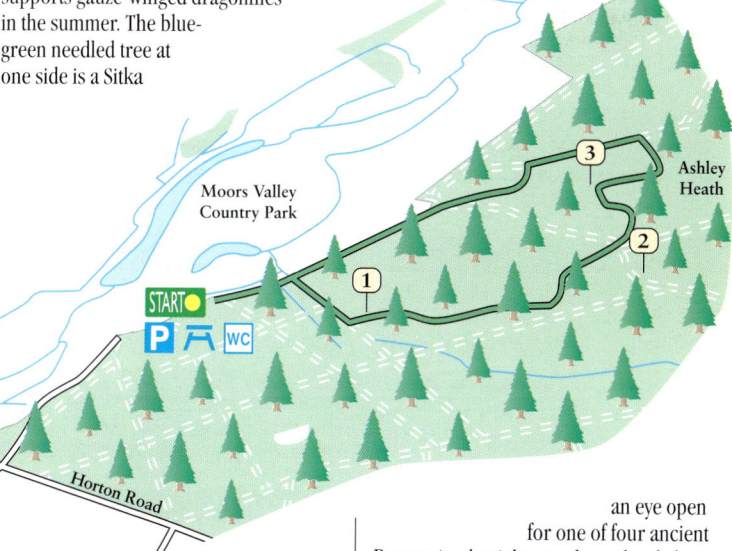

DORSET

Ramsdown Forest Nature Reserve

RAMSDOWN FOREST WALK

Grade	
Distance	1½ miles (2.4km)
Timing	40 mins
Footwear	
Waymarker	Follow red waymarker
Parking	FC Ramsdown Forest car park

Start point The car park entrance is off the Hurn to Sopley road (Avon causeway), just past the lay-by next to a leisure centre, roughly 330ft (100m) from the small roundabout in Hurn village. Look for the map board at the far end of the car park; the first waymarker is inside the forest gateway.

Ramsdown was purchased by the Forestry Commission in 1952, having been used extensively for military purposes between 1939 and 1945. The walk traverses much of Ramsdown Forest Nature Reserve, which is situated immediately south of Hurn Forest, and is mostly flat with only one hill, where there are several steps. A number of areas are managed by conservation groups which protect the valuable habitats here.

The route takes you up a gentle hill towards a commanding series of views from the plateau. Starting with a gentle incline through mixed conifer and birch, the trail then leads up through an open area cleared of invading rhododendron which in the past smothered the heath. This marks the edge of the SSSI (**1**). Removal of the rhododendrons has allowed heather to begin to re-establish itself, so please keep to the paths provided to prevent erosion.

The path zigzags upwards with scattered birch creating little copses. From the plateau (**2**), there are far-reaching views facing north to the airport, Hurn Forest, Ringwood and the New Forest. The trail crosses the plateau, passing oak and birch and also an old radio installation. Well-established heather crowns the hilltop and covers the slopes in shades of purple during the summer, and together with the presence of associated scarce animals such as the smooth snake is the main reason why this area is designated a Forest Nature Reserve.

Top of the hill at Ramsdown – the edge of the SSSI recently cleared of rhododendrons.

WALK 2

Take in the scene from the sturdy viewing deck (**3**), commanding views of Bournemouth, the River Stour and the Isle of Wight. A panorama board helps to pinpoint prominent features from this bird's-eye viewpoint.

The delicate heathy hillside below is managed by the Dorset Wildlife Trust and the deck protects it from being eroded by hundreds of feet. Along the eastern edge of the hill you will see fencing where you will sometimes see roe deer. Rhododendrons which were planted in the last century as cover for game birds and to adorn gardens have become a serious nuisance, smothering both the timber crop and open heath. Foresters and conservationists are doing their best to keep it under control, but it is a never-ending battle.

protecting an area which is managed by the Herpetological (reptiles) Conservation Trust.

Take the winding steps to the left of the platform on to flat terrain, then head out across open land, which is also going to become re-established heathland in due course. The route continues through trees which were planted in the 1950s and '60s

There are several reminders around here of the area's military associations from World War II, notably in the form of concrete footings and roads.

The trail continues on sandy tracks and through mixed conifer, predominantly Maritime pine and Scots pine planted in the early 1960s, then runs back to the car park, rejoining the start of the route.

DORSET

Wareham Forest

THE SIKA TRAIL
Grade	
Distance	3½ miles (5.6km)
Timing	2 hrs
Footwear	
Directions	Follow red waymarker
Parking	FC Sika Trail car park

Start point The entrance is off the Wareham to Bere Regis road, 1 mile (1.6km) north of Wareham and the railway line (take the flyover across the railway line). The access road is almost 1,000ft (330m) long. Look for the map board at the far end of the car park; the first waymarker is to its right.

Wareham Forest was planted in the 1930s and '50s with predominantly Corsican, Scots, Lodgepole and Maritime pine, which are able to thrive on the poor, thin soils. The terrain is flat and dominated by Morden Bog, although paths are dry underfoot. The Sika Trail is in the southern half of the forest, which is leased from the Morden Estate on a 123-year lease. About half of the walk is on open ground due to the bog and areas which have been opened for heathland restoration.

Walking the trail in an anti-clockwise direction you first pass through mature Corsican pine forest planted in 1951, with silver birch in the glades. An unexpected open view looking south reveals rolling farmland and in the distance gravel quarries (**1**), a predominant industry in the area. The former quarry on the right is now managed by the British Herpetological (reptiles) Trust.

The trail continues along the forest edge sheltered by willows, with a small area of oaks on the left, a remnant of cultivated land. Open land now lies ahead with views over a golf course and Morden Bog (**2**). The bog provides a contrast of colour through the seasons and is a National Nature Reserve containing bog myrtle and bog asphodel.

Part of the Sika Trail – Herpetologists will find much to interest them at Wareham.

On both sides of the bog, extensive areas have been permanently cleared of trees so that the scarce heath can re-establish itself. All six British reptile species are found here, including smooth snakes and sand lizards.

Keep a watch out for specially dug ponds (**3**) where dragonflies flit during the summer months, and a dark, gloomy hollow with alder and willows standing in still water. You now pass two Bronze Age burial mounds (**4**) marked with the letter 'M' on posts; they were constructed when the landscape was open heath and were visible for miles.

reddish with spots in summer, and lie up in the denser thickets during the day.

The trail winds on through grand old Monterey pines (**6**) planted in 1933. Pause for a while and marvel at these huge specimens, whose huge cones and dark, fissured trunks lend a cathedral-like atmosphere to the wood. Bird and bat boxes have been installed to provide artificial nesting 'holes' for species such as blue, great and coal tits. Treecreepers and green and greater spotted woodpeckers are common here.

The trail passes amongst Scots and Corsican pine, loops through an old arboretum with its variety of trees and then passes tall, red-trunked Scots pines ideal for crossbills. A belt of oak, birch, willow and hawthorn a little further on marks an old hedge boundary and ditch, a remnant of field systems from a century ago. You then return to the car park, the former site of a gravel quarry.

Soon you pass a stone monument (**5**) dedicated to a forester who battled to grow pines in the water-logged fringes of the bog during the 1950s and '60s. Keep an eye open here for Sika deer, an Asiatic species introduced into Britain 100 years ago. They have dark coats in winter,

DORSET

Affpuddle Forest

RED WALK
Grade	▲
Distance	1¾miles (2.8km)
Timing	1 hr
Footwear	👟
Waymarker	Follow red waymarker
Parking	FC Affpuddle Heath car park and picnic place

Start point Take the B3390 off the A35 Bere Regis to Dorchester road, through Affpuddle. Turn left at a minor crossroad south of Affpuddle (not Waddock Cross, but 1 mile/1.6km north of it). The car park is on the right. The first waymarker is located at the end of the car park by the viewpoint.

Affpuddle, Pallington and Moreton are neighbouring forests that were bought by the Forestry Commission in the 1960s, having previously been leasehold. Affpuddle Forest contains predominantly Corsican pine, the drier ground being on a plateau below which the land is dominated by wet flushes and bog systems. There is remnant heath in open areas. The walk is flat except for one steep hill, and the lower section can be wet in winter.

The trail starts by heading towards the viewpoint, then down an incline alongside the road. Pass a belt of birch and hawthorn, sheltering the track from the road, and continue amongst Corsican pine planted in the 1950s.

The top of the Bronze Age burial mound (**1**) up on the hill on the left has been cleared of trees. Continuing, join the gravel track towards the clearing ahead, where the plants attract many butterflies. Dragonfly nymphs and pondskaters may be seen in the deep drains on the left.

Beyond the clearing the climb uphill is fairly steep but not long, the open sky beyond the trees at the top marking the northern boundary to follow.

Cullpepper's Dish car park is now visible – have a look at Cullpepper's Dish (**2**), on the road edge opposite the car park entrance (take care!). This circular depression is about 100ft (30m) deep and 260ft (80m) wide and is thought to have been created by acidic water eroding the underlying chalk. The shape is akin to a bowl used by herbalists – Nicholas Culpeper was a famous 17th-century herbalist. There are several such depressions in the area, though mostly smaller than this one.

(Note: do not venture beyond the roadside without getting permission from the owner first, since on this side of the road the wood is privately owned.)

Views of Chaldon Down, Winfrith and the Purbeck Hills precede another barrow (**3**), from where the trail descends across open heath and through tall trees – look for the bat boxes which have been put up for Long-eared bats to use as nurseries during the summer.

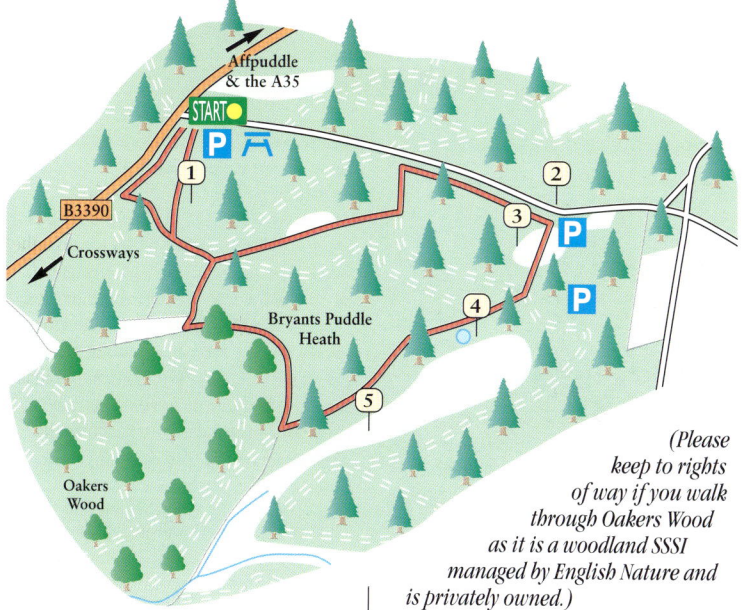

You now join a bridleway once used by horse-drawn coaches. It cuts deeply into the hillside, creating a sunken lane. Below lies the perfectly circular Rimsmoor Pond (**4**; which is actually a peat bog), a SSSI which is 65ft (20m) deep, so take care not to venture on to it. Many unusual bog plants including sundew grow on its surface, along with Sphagnum moss, and a coach and horses are reputed to be lost in its depths.

Beyond the pond, the open area on the left through trees is a wet heathland SSSI (**5**) managed as a conservation area by Forest Enterprise. The trail passes scattered red oaks and bird cherry trees before continuing along an ancient woodland boundary called Oakers Wood as it contains many grand old oaks.

(Please keep to rights of way if you walk through Oakers Wood as it is a woodland SSSI managed by English Nature and is privately owned.)

To the right the ground is open due to the overhead cables, so look out for birds of prey – buzzards and even an occasional hen harrier can be seen in winter. You now cross open, dry heathy ground to where the trail intersects the outward route and runs up a gentle hill back to the car park.

The 65ft deep Rimsmoor Pond is home to several rare plants and is designated a SSSI.

DORSET

Neroche Forest

CASTLE NEROCHE FOREST TRAIL

Grade	
Distance	Whole walk 1½ miles (2.4km). Short route 1 mile (1.6km)
Timing	Whole walk 45 mins Short route 30 mins
Footwear	
Waymarker	Follow red waymarker
Parking	FC Car Park

Start point From Taunton town centre, take the B3170 signposted Corfe. Cross the M5 and after 820ft (250m) take the first left signposted Staple Fitzpaine. Carry on for about 6 miles (9.6km), passing through Staple Fitzpaine to a T-junction. Turn left and then next left at the sign for Castle Neroche Forest Trail. The car park, which lies within the old earth ramparts of Castle Neroche, is a short distance up this road. The walk starts from the noticeboard, from where the first waymarker is visible.

A wintry spectacle from the picnic site at lofty Neroche on the edge of the Black Hills.

Castle Neroche Forest Trail winds through mixed woodland below a dramatic pre-Norman earthwork castle. At 900ft (272m) above sea level, Castle Neroche itself commands extensive views of the Tone valley, Sedgemoor and the farmland of Dorset and Wiltshire. The forest marks the eastern edge of the Blackdown Hills AONB. The walk has some short, steep climbs and steps, and there are steep drops which are protected by fencing, but children should be kept under control.

The trail starts from a dramatic viewpoint (**1**) which looks northwards towards the Quantock Hills and beyond to the Bristol Channel and South Wales. Immediately below are Castle Plantation and the Vale of Taunton. To the right the flat marshes of Sedgemoor stretch away to the sea. On a clear day you can see six counties: Devon, Somerset, Dorset, Wiltshire, Gwent and South Glamorgan. From here the walk crosses an earth bank and continues beside an old beech hedgebank typical of Somerset and Devon.

A short spur to the right takes you to (**2**), another fine view taking in parts of Somerset and Dorset with Glastonbury Tor in the distance. You can see that the trees often grow on hilltops where the ground is less suitable for farming. Retrace your steps then continue down the narrow gully into a beech plantation, where you'll notice damage caused by roe deer rubbing or browsing (nibbling the trees).

WALK 5

Higher up you may see stripped bark – evidence of grey squirrel feeding. Compare how dark it is here when the beech is in leaf with areas of other broadleaves such as oak and birch which you will come across further on.

At (**3**) you look out over Castle Farm. From here the trail follows a bridleway with a stone surface, which has been improved for local farmers. After leaving the road turn left up into the woodland again through mixed tubes used to protect young broadleaved trees. These help the tree to grow quickly and make it easier to find amongst the weeds. You are now at the foot of a steep earth bank and have the same view that would have faced would-be attackers of Castle Neroche.

After leaving the road the trail passes through a variety of conifers and climbs steeply up to the *motte*, a round mound that marked the ultimate castle stronghold.

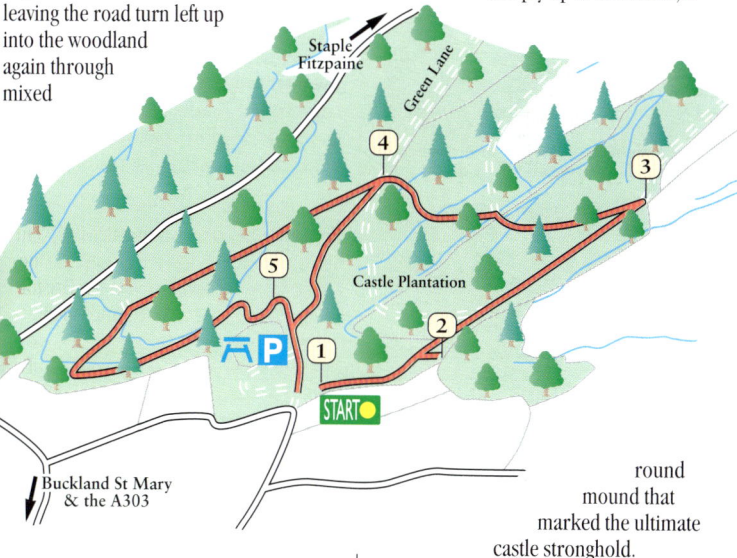

conifer and broadleaves. These were planted in the 1960s and you can see how much faster the conifers have grown than the broadleaves.

At (**4**) join a wide forest road, designed to carry the lorries which transport timber out of the forest. (You can return from here to the car park in under 10 minutes if you wish.) Follow the trail away from the road up the hill, where you can see

Here at the castle there are fine views over Somerset (**5**). The castle dates from 1052 when the outermost of the earth ramparts were built. Taken by Norman knights in 1067, it was abandoned as a residential castle in 1087. Sand and gravel working in the 19th century broke up some of the remaining ramparts, to leave what remains today.

Return to the car park passing a farm which has been here for over 200 years.

SOMERSET

Quantock Forest

RED WALK
Grade	
Distance	2¼ miles (3.6km)
Timing	1¼ hrs
Footwear	
Waymarker	Follow red waymarker
Parking	FC car park at Rams Combe

Start point From Bridgwater follow the A39 toward Watchet but take the turning to Over Stowey just past the Cottage Inn Public House, roughly 3 miles (4.8km) from Cannington. Go straight on at the Marsh Mills crossroad and take the second turning on the left. At Adscombe Farm, follow the forest road for just under 1½ miles (2.4km) to the Rams Combe car park. The walk starts from the noticeboard, from where the first waymarker is visible.

Set within a 38 sq mile (99 sq km) Area of Outstanding Natural Beauty, Quantock Forest stretches over 1,554 acres (629 ha) of hills and steep-sided combes near Nether Stowey in Somerset. Records show that these hills have been covered by forests for centuries and the timber produced has been used for charcoal-making and shipbuilding amongst countless other uses. Today the hills are owned by Somerset County Council but managed on a 999-year lease by the Forestry Commission. Tree species include oak, Douglas fir, Sitka spruce and larch. The walk explores some of the secluded combes and challenging hills in this beautiful area of forest, with the chance of wildlife, particularly red deer, round every bend.

Starting from the main Rams Combe car park the route heads out following the small stream which flows through Rams Combe. This stream is crossed as the walk turns left and there follows a steep climb to West Hill, at 900ft (275m) the highest point on the trail.

Quantock Forest offers many opportunities to spot wildlife, especially red deer.

28   WALK 6

The route runs down from West Hill and at (**1**) you'll see sessile oak trees growing with bilberry beneath them. Oak makes excellent charcoal and would have been managed by coppicing in the past. The word 'sessile' means unstalked, referring to the acorns.

Leaving the forest road there is a climb to Lord's Ball (a specific hill in the Quantocks), which is around 820ft (250m) above sea level, before a steep drop down on to another forest road.

At (**2**) there is an old quarry where you can see the red Devonian sandstone that makes up these hills. This is called 'Hangmans Grit' and it was used to help build the forest roads.

The path turns sharply left at (**3**) and some large, widely-spaced Douglas firs can be seen further up the valley. These trees are the remains of a much denser crop which has been very heavily thinned to leave those you see, 100-115ft (30-35m) apart. Many of the seeds they produce will grow to form the next crop, meaning that replanting will not be necessary – such is 'natural regeneration'.

You are now in Quantock Combe which the trail follows downhill to the Seven Wells car park. On the way it is possible to see muddy hollows on the banks of the stream to the left. These are wallows made by deer. At (**4**) there is a field which is managed as a deer lawn and red deer can sometimes be seen here in large numbers.

From the Seven Wells car park turn left and walk uphill along the forest road back to Rams Combe car park.

SOMERSET

Ashclyst Forest

RED TRAIL

Grade	▲
Distance	2½ miles (4km)
Timing	1¼ hrs
Footwear	👟
Waymarker	Follow red waymarker
Parking	Forest Gate car park

Start point: From Exeter take the B3181 through Broadclyst village towards Cullompton. Just under 2 miles (3.2km) from Broadclyst turn right, signed Ashclyst and Caddihoe. Forest Gate car park is on the left after 1¼ miles (2km). The walk starts from the noticeboard, from where the first waymarker is visible.

Largely planted at the beginning of the 19th century by Sir Thomas Acland, Ashclyst covers the highest point in the National Trust's Killerton Estate and is managed jointly by the National Trust and Forest Enterprise. Ashclyst is renowned for its wildlife, in particular its butterflies. The walk starts near the highest point of the forest and heads gradually downhill to the forest edge, which it follows for some way before climbing slowly back to the car park. Passing through much broadleaved woodland, the walk changes with each season but is at its best in spring and early summer.

Leaving the car park and following the grassy forest paths you pass through a great variety of tree and shrub species before emerging on to one of the most important conservation areas in Ashclyst.

The Powerline Butterfly Meadows (**1**) are managed to encourage the plants on which butterflies thrive, and it is possible in summer to see most of the 30 or so species which breed in the forest. July is the best month with White Admiral, Silver-washed Fritillary, Marbled White and Purple Hairstreak on the wing. Leaving the Powerline you can reach the edge of the forest through a mixture of beech, larch and Scots pine. The trail keeps to the forest edge for some way offering views to the south: at

A pied flycatcher, one of the summer visitors to Ashclyst, brings food for its young.

(**2**) towards Exeter Airport, while from (**3**) Broadclyst is the nearest village, and beyond that Exeter, with the Haldon Hills on the skyline.

The southern edge of the woodland contains some of the oldest trees in the forest. Several oaks have been pollarded (one or two as recently as the early 1990s) and others, on the boundary bank, have been laid but have since grown up into large trees.

Pollarding involves cutting the top off the tree 6-7ft (2m) above the ground, with the resultant new growth being used for various wood products. Laying, meanwhile, is a traditional technique whereby living stems are cut close to ground level, with the remaining stems being bent over and woven together to form a living barrier, which continues to grow.

At Point (**4**) the forest canopy is dominated by ash which thrive on the damp edges of the small stream here and, along with the word 'clyst', meaning a stream, lend themselves to the forest's name. In winter woodcock can be found around here.

Eventually you leave the forest edge and turn up through broadleaved trees before entering a mixture of Corsican pine and Sitka spruce. This is followed by a section along a forestry road, passing two forest cottages (**5**) on the right, both painted in the Killerton yellow ochre. In early summer keep a lookout for pied flycatchers in the big oaks. They are migratory visitors from Africa.

Soon after the cottages the route turns right and leads back to the car park.

DEVON

Stoke Woods

RED TRAIL
Grade
Distance 1½ miles (2.4km)
Timing 45 mins
Footwear
Waymarker Follow red waymarker
Parking FC car park

Start point Head north out of Exeter on the A377 Crediton road until the Cowley Bridge roundabout, then take the A396, signed for Tiverton, for ½ mile (0.8km). The car park is on the right. The walk starts from the noticeboard, from where the first waymarker is visible.

Stoke Woods lie just within the City of Exeter's northern boundary and overlook the River Exe from the north-facing slope of Stoke Hill. The forest is made up of conifers planted mostly in the 1950s and broadleaved trees (mainly oak), some of which are over 150 years old. The woods are extremely attractive and valuable for wildlife, and have been an SSSI since 1986. The walk follows the hillside after the short climb from the car park, taking in both broadleaved and conifer trees of varying ages. It is a quiet walk with a potential abundance of wildlife.

The trail initially climbs a narrow gully following a tiny stream flanked with western hemlock and mixed broadleaves including Wych elm, before emerging into a stand of large oak (**1**). These are widely spaced with grassy glades beneath them and form a seed orchard where acorns are collected to be grown in Forest Enterprise tree nurseries. The plant life growing on the ground here is worth comparing with that found further along the trail.

Continue through the wood and on across the slope, where there are a lot of coppiced trees, mainly hazel and sycamore (**2**). Coppicing is an ancient

A high level, oak-framed view of the River Exe winding away from Stoke Hill.

WALK 8

method of managing broadleaved woodland whereby trees are felled and allowed to regrow for several years. This produces a large number of stems from the same root system, which are cut when they have reached the desired size and used for a number of purposes.

The trees growing at (**3**) are larch, a deciduous conifer which allows large amounts of light to reach the forest floor, again encouraging a varied ground flora. Look out also for the climbing honeysuckle.

Dropping on to a forest track which leads towards the eastern end of the hill, there are Douglas firs on the right and oaks on the left. Cut down to cross another small stream at (**4**), where in early summer golden saxifrage, dogs mercury and the aromatic wild garlic cover the stream's banks with triangular stemmed sedges numerous all year.

Following the stream, alder is the most common tree, thriving on the damp soils.

At (**5**) Lawson cypresses grow on the downhill side of the track, with oak on the uphill. This oak would have been coppiced once but has more recently been 'singled'. This means that instead of allowing lots of stems to grow, the best have been selected and nurtured to become trees in their own right. The ground flora here contrasts with that seen earlier: wood-rush is the most common species and the heather and bilberry indicate poor soils.

The path runs back to the car park above the River Exe and past a viewpoint (**6**) overlooking the river and surrounding countryside, passing just wide of the edge of the wood.

DEVON

Eggesford Wood

TAW VALLEY RED WALK

Grade	▲
Distance	0.8 mile (1.3km)
Timing	40 mins
Footwear	👟
Waymarker	Follow red waymarker
Parking	FC car park

Start point The car park is signposted from the A377 just south of Eggesford. The walk starts at a large starter post with yellow markings easily seen from the car park.

The first trees planted by the Forestry Commission were at Eggesford, on 8 December 1919. This walk takes in the Taw valley, which is a very rich and diverse habitat for birds, mammals and insects. The most important inhabitant is the wild otter of 'Tarka' fame, but the woodlands higher up the valley sides are home to red and roe deer, with dormice nesting in the hazel coppice. Green woodpeckers and nuthatch can also be found in

34   WALK 9

The Queen's Stone commemorating Her Majesty's visit in 1956 to mark the planting of 1 million acres of trees.

these woods, and foresters are seeking to encourage more birds by putting up nesting boxes in suitable locations, where natural nesting sites are not available.

The trail climbs steadily away from the start up a narrow track to the edge of the wood. Turn left at this point, down an earth track through a young Douglas fir plantation. At the bottom you will join a forest road from where there is a view (**1**) through the large Douglas firs of the Taw valley with the river and Tarka line below.

The trail descends to the left down a forest track giving you a close-up of 75-year-old Douglas firs (**2**), which were amongst the first to be planted by the Forestry Commission. Some of these are well over 100ft (30m) tall and it is an awesome experience to walk amongst them. Once at the bottom of this track follow the trail past the field boundaries leading back to the car park.

At the car park have a look at the Queen's Stone (**3**), down towards the road. The stone and the adjacent trees commemorate the visit of Her Majesty Queen Elizabeth II to Eggesford on 8 May 1956, to mark the planting of 1 million acres (404,700 ha) of trees by the Forestry Commission.

DEVON

Eggesford Wood

HEYWOOD RED WALK
Grade
Distance 2½ miles (4km)
Timing 2 hrs
Footwear
Waymarker Follow red waymarker
Parking FC car park at the entrance to the wood

Start point Turn off the A377 at Eggesford Station and cross the River Taw. Turn right following signs to Wembworthy and then right again after 1 mile (1.6km). Go past the Wembworthy Centre and continue to the Forestry Commission car park, which is on the right after 0.8 mile (1.3km). The walk starts at the large square post by the barrier.

These woodlands are in one of the most beautiful parts of Devon and offer good views of the glorious countryside from several vantage points along the walk, including the top of a Norman motte and bailey.

From the car park there are good views across the Devon countryside and the vineyard on the opposite slope. The walk initially follows the hard road through young plantations of Douglas fir and then descends a grass track through mature Douglas firs to a fine specimen Douglas (**1**) that measures over 23ft (7m) in diameter and is about 125 years old. This area is

The massive Douglas fir which dominates the others on this walk.

WALK 10

worth exploring as there are several other specimen trees including a number of large Monkey Puzzles.

The trail leads on to a Norman motte and bailey (**2**), an ancient fort which occupies a small rise from where there are superb views of the Taw valley. From here you pass through young plantations and go back on to hard road.

After crossing the highway follow the valley bottom along the forest road (**3**) – a good area to spot butterflies during the summer months. There is a steep section at the end of this part of the trail that can get quite muddy, but once at the top the route returns to the tarmac road.

This is a particularly lovely part of the walk offering pleasant views out over the surrounding countryside, which has been widely promoted through the popular Tarka Project – a Devon County Council initiative which has been devised to encourage conservation, recreation and tourism in Northern Devon. Much of the countryside around here remains unchanged since the time when Henry Williamson found inspiration in it for his classic novel *Tarka the Otter*.

Follow the tarmac road back to the car park, but please remember that this is a public road.

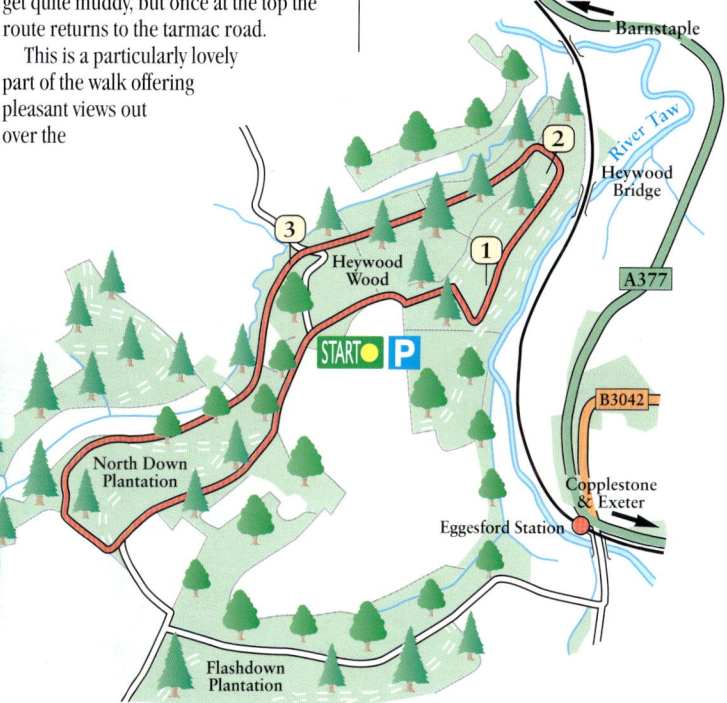

DEVON

Abbeyford Wood

YELLOW WALK

Grade	
Distance	2 miles (3.2km)
Timing	1½ hrs
Footwear	
Waymarker	Follow yellow waymarker
Parking	FC car park at the entrance to Abbeyford Wood

Start point Abbeyford Wood is 2 miles (3.2km) north of Okehampton. The car park is signed off the county highway running through the wood. The start of the waymarked walk is a large square post.

These are very diverse woodlands with spectacular views across to Dartmoor. The featured walk is an easy circular route (the route described below goes clockwise) and can be followed in either direction, passing through newly planted woodlands and more mature plantations, with much diversity of both scenery and wildlife.

Following the yellow waymarker posts from the car park, the trail takes you down to the public highway. This is not a busy road but take care when crossing.

Superbly camouflaged, secretive and rare nightjars inhabit these woods.

38   WALK 11

You now enter a wood (**1**) known as Springetts, where you will see the remnants of the large Douglas fir trees that covered this whole area until the big windblow of 1990 when the wood was devastated. Replanting has taken place with Douglas fir and a lot of fresh habitats have been provided for many bird species including the nightjar, with the whole (**2**) whilst on your right you will notice there are mixed plantations of Douglas fir, larch and young birch.

At the moment, you are walking on part of the long distance Tarka Trail. This is 180 miles (290km) long and joins Dartmoor to Exmoor and the North Devon coast. The theme for the trail is taken from Henry Williamson's classic novel *Tarka the Otter*. Set and written in the area it tells the story of a young otter's life and travel.

area being a good hunting ground for buzzards and Tawny owls.

After circling the newly planted woodland, the trail leads back on to the highway. Turn left here and then right back into Abbeyford Wood. As you follow the hard, wide road you will have spectacular views across on to Dartmoor

Following the yellow waymarker posts the walk now rises gently, again on hard surface all the way, passing through mature larch plantations with remnants of oak plantations dating from 1880. You then return to the car park, the older, more mature woodlands a huge contrast to the newly replanted Springetts Wood.

DEVON

Haldon Forest

RED TRAIL - THE LONG WALK

Grade	
Distance	8¾ miles (14km)
Timing	4 hrs
Footwear	
Waymarker	Follow red waymarkers
Parking	FC car park at Bullers Hill

Start point Turn off the A38 Exeter/Plymouth Road at the top of Haldon Hill signposted Exeter Racecourse and head towards Dunchideock for just over 1 mile (1.6km). Bullers Hill car park is just over 300ft (100m) beyond the FC offices. The walk starts from the bottom end of the car park.

The Haldon Ridge – sometimes referred to as 'Devon's Forgotten Hills'– offers superb scenery and a tremendous variety of wildlife, assets which were recognised in 1992 when much of the forest was designated a SSSI by English Nature. The Red Trail starts from one of the highest points on the ridge (around 800ft/250m above sea level) on Bullers Hill and takes in some of the most interesting parts, but includes some steep slopes.

Initially the red, green and blue trails run together; the blue then splits off and soon afterwards so does the green (**1**). The red route then crosses the Trusham road and enters Lucy Ball Plantation, named after a local farmer's daughter, before dropping into the Ashton valley with France Brook at the bottom. To the right (**2**) the Lawrence Tower (Haldon Belvedere) can be seen. Renovated in 1995 this impressive three-turreted tower dates from 1788, having been built as a memorial to General Stringer Lawrence by Sir Robert Palk, a Governor of Madras who owned an 11,000-acre (4,450 ha) estate around Haldon and the Teign valley.

From (**3**) you can see Hennock village, while Ashton and the Church of St John the Baptist are in the valley below (**4**).

A fabulous panorama of Dartmoor from the Bird of Prey Viewpoint.

Cross the Trusham road again and descend the hill to pass under the powerline and over the small Bramble Brook before turning up Long Ride, with a crop of Sitka spruce to the right.

Leaving Long Ride (**5**), follow an old field boundary containing hazel, oak and hawthorn – a typical habitat for dormice. The trail then joins with the blue walk and runs along

Now follow a short section alongside the highway before turning right into Tower Wood. There is an option here to return to the car park (**9**). After the superb view to the Exe Estuary (**10**), continue around the hill, recross the

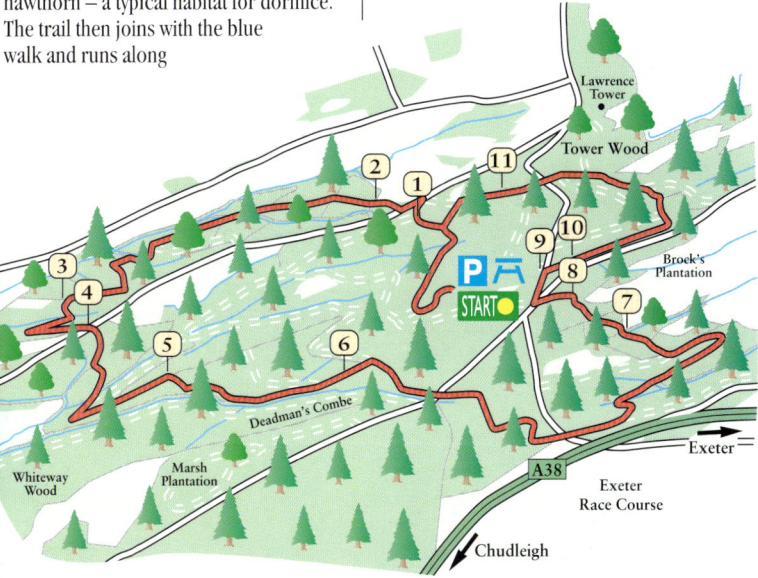

Deadman's Combe, the grisly name referring to what was a burial ground during the Plague.

As you climb back to the top of the ridge you pass a pond (**6**) which attracts dragonflies in summer. Having crossed the Old Chudleigh road you reach the Dunchideock road near the racecourse before dropping down the other side of the hill on to a forest road with views to Exeter (**7** and **8**).

Dunchideock road and head downhill. An access path (**11**) leads to the Bird of Prey Viewpoint, which offers stunning views over Dartmoor, Haytor and the Teign valley. Summer is the best time to see the birds, especially hobby, Honey buzzard and goshawk. There are interpretation points explaining more about the birdlife of Haldon at the viewpoint

The red trail now joins the green trail again for the walk back to Bullers Hill.

DEVON 41

Haldon Forest

MAMHEAD ALL ABILITIES TRAIL

Grade	
Distance	1 mile (1.6km)
Timing	30 mins
Footwear	
Waymarker	Follow the surfaced path from car park
Parking	FC car park at Mamhead

Start point Turn off the A380 Torbay/Exeter road on to the B3381 at Mamhead Cross and after 1 mile (1.6km) take the first right towards Ashcombe. The Mamhead car park is on the left after ½ mile (0.8km). The walk starts from the noticeboard, from where the first waymarker is visible.

Haldon Forest covers some 3,500 acres (1,400 ha) of the Haldon Ridge and supports many tree species. The area around Mamhead has mainly pine and spruce trees, which are well suited to the soils of this area. The All Abilities Trail is level, with a surfaced path which is suitable for wheelchairs and pushchairs. Benches are placed around the trail as rest points and picnic tables are sited on the viewpoint. Watch out for fallow and roe deer in the woodlands, and for siskins and crossbills searching for food in the trees on the edge of the trail.

From the car park head east following the line of an old deer wall used to keep deer in the Mamhead Estate grounds. Beech, Sweet chestnut and Scots pine give an avenue-like appearance to the route. The young broadleaf trees growing at (**1**) are an oak/cherry mix and precede the opening at (**2**) from where you

Picnickers relax and enjoy the wide-angle view towards the coast.

WALK 13

can enjoy one of the best views in Devon. The hill drops away sharply in front of the viewpoint towards agricultural land, the Exe estuary and the coast. The sandspit of Dawlish Warren Nature Reserve is clearly visible and Exmouth is the town on the far side of the Exe, with the white buildings at Lympstone to the left. On a clear day it is even possible to see Portland Bill in the distance, on the coast.

Immediately below the viewpoint to the left is the impressive Mamhead House, which in its present form dates from 1828, while to the right is an obelisk dating from 1742.

Turning left from the viewpoint the trail follows a wide forest road which is mainly made of flint, the stone which caps the Haldon Hills.

The walk turns left again at (**3**) into Tebbit's Copse, a special area of broadleaf plantation which was initiated in 1993 when Lady Tebbit opened the trail. A wide variety of trees have since been planted here by families and individuals to commemorate the occasion.

Beyond Tebbit's Copse you enter a Sitka spruce plantation which dates from 1994, the previous crop of Corsican pine having been blown down in the storms of January 1990, which inflicted much damage on local woods.

The path back to the car park adjoins the road verges which are ablaze in summer with purple heather.

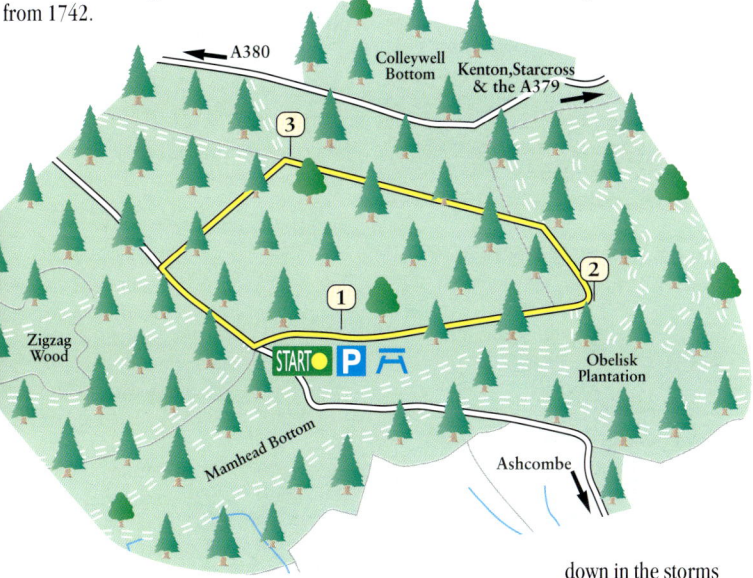

Constructed from Portland stone it stands 100ft (30m) high and was used as a navigational aid for shipping clearly visible from many miles out to sea.

DEVON 43

Haldon Forest

THE BUTTERFLY WALK
Grade
Distance 2¼ miles (3.6km)
Timing 1½ hrs
Footwear
Waymarker Follow green waymarker
Parking FC car park at Bullers Hill

Start point Turn off the A38 Exeter/Plymouth road at the top of Haldon Hill signposted Exeter Racecourse and head towards Dunchideock for just over 1 mile (1.6km). Bullers Hill car park is on the left about 300ft (100m) beyond the FC offices. The walk starts from the bottom end of the car park.

Haldon Forest is one of Devon's most important wildlife areas. Much of it is designated a SSSI because it is a nationally important habitat for breeding and hunting birds of prey (7 species are regularly recorded during the summer). It also supports a very high population of nightjars and more than 30 species of butterfly. The walk takes in some of the warmer south- and south-west facing slopes of the ridge, which offer ideal conditions for butterflies and other wildlife, as well as good views towards Dartmoor.

The green trail or 'Butterfly Walk' descends from the car park through a variety of tree species before turning right and emerging on to a forest road. This is Brookes Ride which runs across the hill and follows a spring line (**1**) on the right; this remains wet in all but the driest years. At (**2**) you cross Bramble Brook for the first time before turning left at the top of 'Brookes Spur'.

The wide grassy verges here provide valuable feeding and breeding habitat for several species of butterfly, including Dingy and Grizzled Skipper, Marbled White and Common Blue. At (**3**) there is a view to the village of Hennock nestling on the far side of the Teign valley.

Having left the 'spur' ride, you pass through a mixture of large Scots pine, beech and sycamore before

Late spring usually features the appearance of the rare Pearl-bordered Fritillary.

44   **WALK 14**

emerging on to another forest road at the top of the Powerline Forest Nature Reserve, which is sponsored by the National Grid company. These managed wildflower meadows support several rare species of butterfly, including Wood White, Pearl-bordered Fritillary and Small Pearl-bordered Fritillary, particularly in May and June. Later in the year Ringlets, Meadow Brown, Silver-washed

dug to drain the ground before planting the trees in the extracted soil – a technique called 'dolloping'.

At point (**4**) there is a view back down the track with Hennock again visible, Canonteign Forest to its right and Haytor on the horizon.

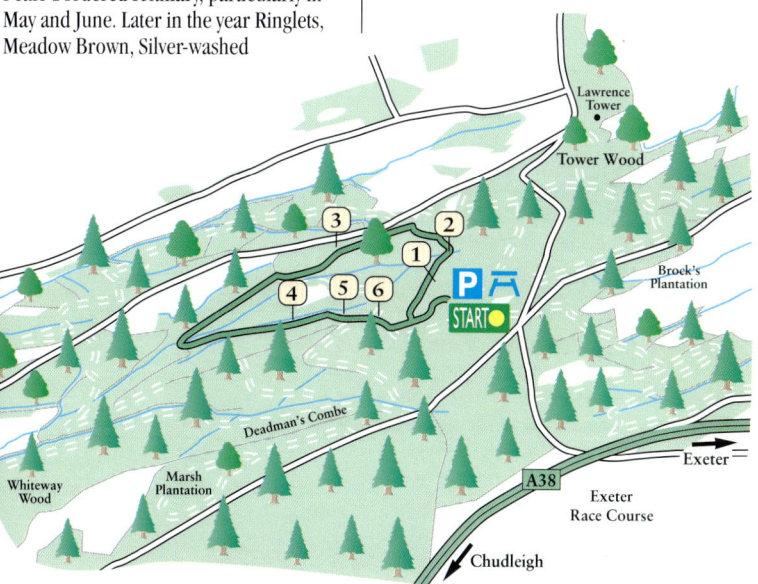

Fritillary and White Admiral may be seen. The meadows are flanked by hedgerows which provide food and cover for birdlife, and fallow deer are also regularly seen here, grazing in the grasslands.

Leaving the Powerline cross the Bramble Brook for a second time before the climb back to Bullers Hill. This track is called 'Horses ride' and for most of its route has young Sitka spruce growing on either side. You can see the wide ditches

The trail passes the ruins of Higher Kiddens Farm at (**5**) where all that remains are some walls and granite gateposts. This farm existed until 1920 when the forest was planted, but the buildings were used until just after World War II to stable the horses used by the foresters for work such as ploughing.

At (**6**) there are some unusual Southern beech trees planted as part of the Queen's Silver Jubilee Celebrations in 1977.

DEVON

Bellever Forest

RED WALK
Grade	▲
Distance	3 miles (4.8km)
Timing	1½ hrs
Footwear	👟
Waymarker	Follow red waymarker
Parking	FC car park at Bellever

Start point Bellever is signposted off the B3212 between Postbridge and Two Bridges. Bellever Forest main car park is 1 mile (1.6km) by road from the B3212. The walk starts from the noticeboard, from where the first waymarker is visible.

Bellever Forest was acquired by the Forestry Commission from the Royal Duchy of Cornwall in 1931. The original planting had been carried out by the Duchy 10 years previously with beech, Sitka spruce, larch and Douglas fir. More broadleaved trees have recently been introduced to enrich the wildlife. The walk follows forest roads and small stoney tracks and crosses rough moorland. This is very much an upland walk with Bellever Tor in view and narrow, fast-flowing brooks.

At the start of the trail there are attractive picnicking areas on the west bank of the East Dart River downstream from the clapper bridge (**1**). Clapper bridges are a feature of Dartmoor which were constructed by laying huge slabs of unwrought granite on granite piers and buttresses. They were probably built by farm settlers and are mostly on the line of packhorse tracks

As the trail climbs out of the valley, Bellever Tor (**2**) appears on the horizon looming over the forest. Rising some 1,456ft (443m) above sea level, it is regarded by many as one of the finest Dartmoor Tors, being less rugged and not so tall as most, and having fine, gentle lines, clearly visible from here.

A 'tor' is explained by geologists as the hard granite core of a higher mountain range of softer rock which has eroded away. From the summit of Bellever Tor the views over Dartmoor National Park are spectacular – on a clear day you can see as far as Fernworthy to the north, Holne Moor to the south, North Hessary Tor to the west and Haytor Rocks to the east.

Running due north from Bellever Tor is Lakehead Newtake (**3**), an area which was inhabited by early man; it is estimated that the population would have been about 2,000. Many stone circles are clearly visible now, and this area has been left unplanted since the 1930s in order to safeguard these remains. Left to natural processes some of the old boundary walls have become completely enveloped in an attractive and highly decorative covering of ling, bilberry, moss and ferns.

Ahead the route joins with the old 'Lichway' (**4**). This ancient trackway running east to west between Lakehead Hill to the north and Bellever Tor to the south was used for various purposes, amongst them to transport the dead for burial at Lydford and as a 'highway' for wedding ceremonies and other such functions.

In our own time, farming plays an integral role in this area, and the track here continues down through Bellever Farm (**5**), where the 'new' granite buildings have become a familiar aspect of the landscape and constitute a kind of living history.

Snowscape above the treeline, viewed from the summit of Bellever Tor.

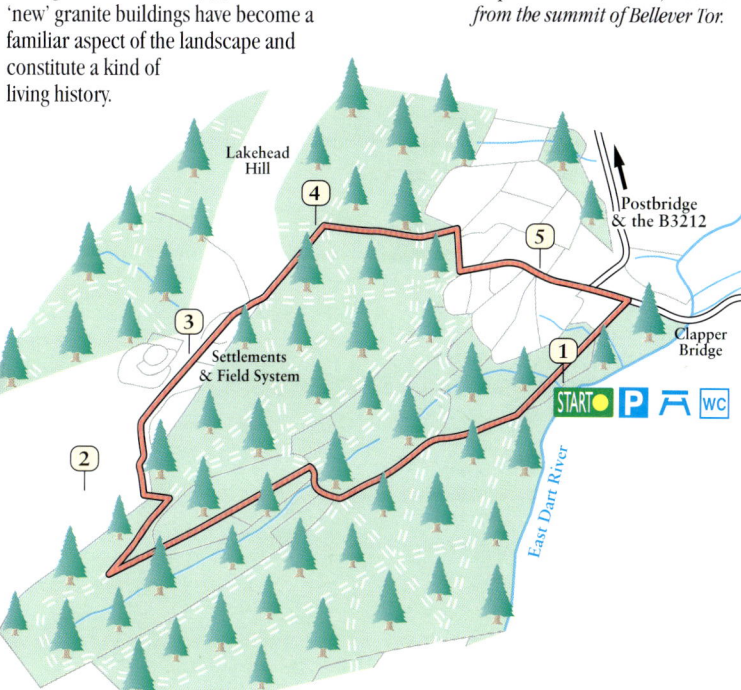

DEVON

47

Fernworthy Forest

RED TRAIL
Grade
Distance   2½ miles (4km)
Timing   1¼ hrs
Footwear
Waymarker Follow red waymarker
Parking   South West Water car park at Fernworthy

Start point From Chagford follow the brown Tourist Route signs to Fernworthy Reservoir.

Fernworthy is the largest forest in Dartmoor National Park, covering 1,423 acres (576 ha) planted on the hills and encompassing the water catchment area for the 91-acre (37 ha) reservoir which feeds the Teign River. The forest, which pre-dates the reservoir by some years (1921 against 1936), is a very productive area yielding quality timber. It has been owned and managed since 1931 by the Forestry Commission having been planted originally by the Duchy of Cornwall.

The start of the Red Trail follows the wide margins of the southern edge of the reservoir. Here the ground is covered with moss, bilberry and ferns, while the most common broadleaved tree is rowan or Mountain ash. When water levels are low, you may be able to see a stone bridge towards the western end of the reservoir. The bridge originally crossed the South Teign River and led to Fernworthy Farm.

The trail soon turns away from the water and follows the road for a short section before heading into the forest. The trees to the left alongside the road (**1**) have been retained by foresters for their landscape value, while growing beneath them – and in other parts of the forest – you will spot many young trees. These have regenerated naturally, with seeds from the older conifers establishing themselves, thus making it unnecessary

Fernworthy Reservoir – surrounded by mixed plantation.

WALK 16

for foresters to replant a crop. Natural regeneration is more successful here than anywhere else on Dartmoor with up to 143,000 trees per hectare being recorded as growing.

A short distance inside the forest the trail crosses Lowton Brook before following another track uphill, eventually emerging into a clearing (**2**) where a number of stone hut circles are marked. These date from between 2,000 and 1,000 BC and great care is taken to protect them. At (**3**) there are more stone circles and an unplanted area which

As the trail descends you cross Assycombe Brook via Tims Bridge before following the stream down beneath some spectacular Douglas fir trees planted in 1923. At (**4**) look out for alders growing on the banks just before you cross another bridge.

The bird hide at (**5**) is owned by South West Water and overlooks a Nature Reserve managed by Devon Birdwatching and Preservation Society. The best season for birdwatchers is winter when visiting birds include pochard, teal and goosander. Migrating osprey have also been recorded.

After leaving the forest and again following a short section on the road, the path turns left along the reservoir and returns to the car park.

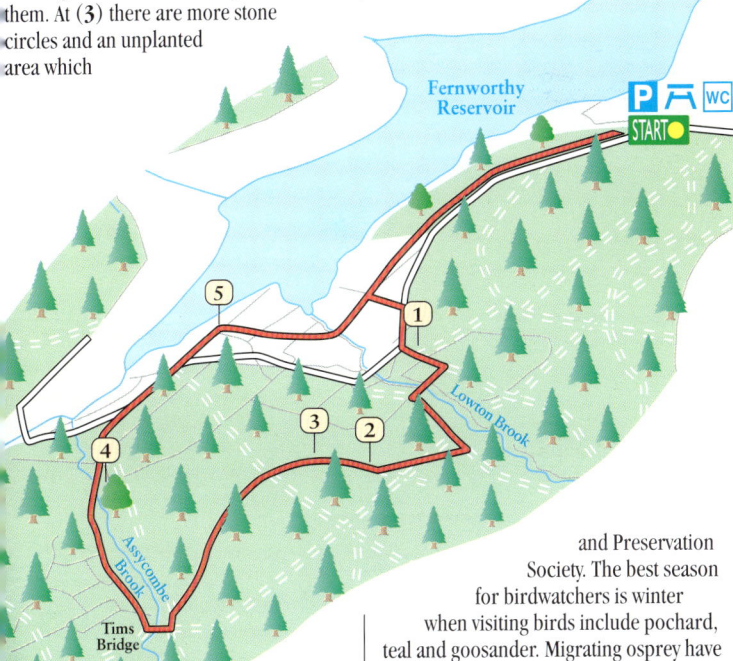

offers good views over the reservoir towards Thornworthy Tor.

DEVON 49

Denham Forest

RED TRAIL

Grade	▲
Distance	2½ miles (4km) Circular Route ½ mile (0.8km) Linear Route
Timing	1 hr Circular Route 20 mins Linear Route
Footwear	👟
Waymarker	Follow red waymarker
Parking	FC car park at Denham

Start point From Tavistock take the A390 towards Gunnislake but turn left at Gulworthy on to the B3257. Just before reaching Bere Alston turn left for Buckland Monachorum. Denham Forest is on the right after a little over 1 mile (1.6km) and before you reach Denham Bridge. The car park is a short distance down the forest road. The walk starts from the noticeboard, from where the first waymarker is visible.

Denham clings to the side of the beautiful, secluded, Tavy valley and occupies land that was once part of the Buckland Abbey Estate but which is now owned by the National Trust and leased by the Forestry Commission. There are commercial conifer plantings here, but also large amounts of broadleaf woodland which contain many tree species. There is one walk which can be divided into two parts: a circular route which leads downstream from the car park and a shorter, linear path which runs upstream to Denham Bridge.

The linear path to Denham Bridge runs from the opposite end of the car park and follows a cart track through oak woodland to meet the county road at the bridge. It takes about 10 minutes in either direction. The bridge has two arches and dates from around the 17th century. *Please take great care if you go on to the bridge as it carries a public road.*

The circular section follows a forest road from the bottom of the car park with the River Tavy a few metres to the left. The trail is surrounded by large broadleaves including oak, sycamore and Sweet chestnut, and hazel and hawthorn can also be found.

The sturdy character of the historic 17th-century Denham Bridge, set amongst mature trees by the Tavy.

50   WALK 17

You soon leave the forest road, forking down to the left closer to the river, where much of the ground flora consists of the grass-like woodrush. The path follows the river and it is occasionally possible to walk out on to stony 'beaches' (**1**) if the water level is low. Keep a sharp lookout for kingfishers.

The track rises slowly, sometimes passing close to the Tavy with glimpses of the forest on the hillside in front and above, making this a very impressive part of the route.

Eventually you leave the river and head right alongside a small stream which is flanked by a crop of Douglas fir (**2**). Watch out for a flat 'rubbery' plant called liverwort; it enjoys the damp conditions found here and grows on both the ground and rocks.

Leaving the stream, the trail returns to the forest road where you turn right back towards the car park. Along the way the road is edged with heather and you can see both sessile and pedunculate oak (**3**). Have a look at the acorns: pedunculate oaks have two or three acorns growing in a cluster on a stalk as opposed to the sessile oak, where the acorns do not grow on a stalk.

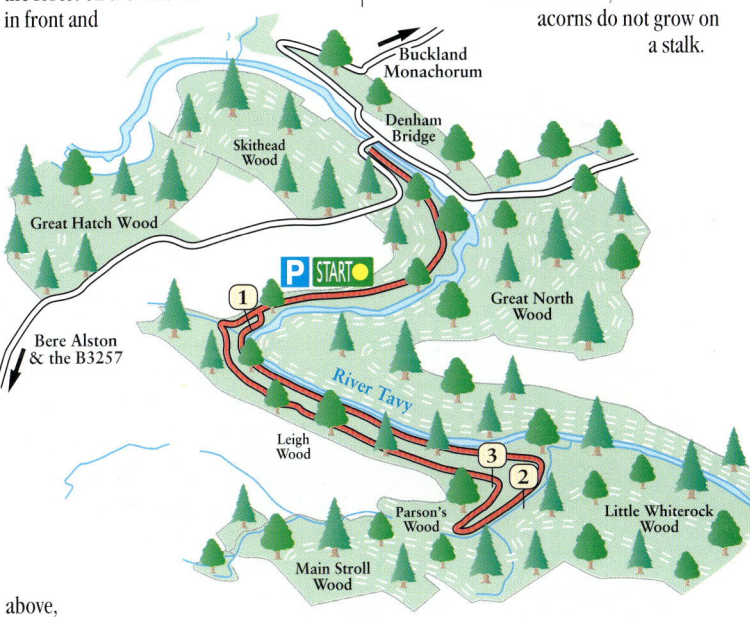

The road follows the contours of the hill, allowing occasional views down to the river or across to the opposite side of the valley.

DEVON

Cann Wood

BLUE TRAIL

Grade	
Distance	2¾ miles (4.4km)
Timing	1½ hrs
Footwear	
Waymarker	Follow blue waymarker
Parking	FC car park at Cann Wood

Start point From the Marsh Mills roundabout on the A38 at Plymouth take the B3416 to Plympton, turn left and cross the railway, following the signs for Boringdon Hall. The car park is on the left approximately 2 miles (3.2km) from Colebrook. The walk starts from the car park.

Woodland has been recorded here since at least the 15th century, when the area lay within what is now the Saltram Estate. Parts of this fascinating area have been mined for silver, there is a disused 19th-century tramway and an Iron Age hill fort lies on the forest edge. For the wildlife enthusiast, buzzards, green and greater spotted woodpeckers, fallow and roe deer are just some of the wildlife species that can be seen. The walk passes through plantations of varying ages and species and is predominantly on high level ground, making walking easy, although it can be muddy, so be prepared to wear waterproof footwear.

WALK 18

The trail starts by heading through a young Douglas fir plantation for a short way before skirting the site of an Iron Age hill fort called Boringdon Camp (**1**). There is a single rampart and views north to Shaugh Prior and north-east to Lee Moor.

The path passes through a mixture of Japanese larch, hazel and sweet chestnut before joining a forest road and turning right. On the left at this junction stands a granite column (**2**) of which little is known. Theories include it being a relic from the days of the estate's ownership or that it was erected to mark the site of the tramway.

A short distance along the forest road the path runs through the supports of a now dismantled bridge (**3**). This was built as part of the Lee Moor Tramway, originally a branch of the Tavistock line, but taken over and rebuilt in 1858 by the Lee Moor China Clay Company to transport clay to Plymouth. Horse-drawn from Marsh Mills to Plym Bridge, the trucks were dragged up the inclines by the force of fully-laden trucks coming downhill. The line was last used in 1947.

Leave the forest road by forking off to the right and, a short distance past the tramway bridge, there is a steep drop at

Often heard, less often seen – a handsome green woodpecker looks for a meal.

(**4**) on the right into the valley. Sweet chestnut grows here, a species native to the Mediterranean islands and introduced into Britain by the Romans.

From here, the trail follows a forest road before heading up a shallow valley with the tramway to the right. This is crossed at (**5**) where the tramway was built in a cutting to reduce the gradient. The path heads back to the car park close to the southern edge of the wood. Keep an eye open for deer tracks along the way.

DEVON

Deerpark Woods

THE DEERPARK TRAIL
Grade
Distance 3½ miles (5.6km)
Timing 2 hrs
Footwear
Directions Follow blue waymarker
Parking FC car park
Start point Turn off the B3359 road, following signs for Herodsfoot and Deerpark. The FC car park is clearly signed. To find the start of the trail, follow the forest road downhill to the starter post.

Red deer stags graze warily in the broadleaved woodland.

Deerpark Woods are planted on the site of an old deer park, and the boundary wall is still visible in places. Today, there are plenty of deer roaming here – both roe and red – and you may be lucky enough to catch a glimpse of one through the trees. You are more likely, though, to spot signs of deer on the edges of the forest roads – deer slots or footprints are often visible in the mud. This trail is a circular route which can be walked in either direction, but the preferred way leads downhill proceeding from the right of the trail starter post.

Shortly after the start of the trail, there are superb views (**1**) of the Herodsfoot valley. All along the trail you will notice the distinctive rosebay willowherb, a herbaceous plant which can grow to over 3ft (1m) in height and which has rose-purple coloured flowers in late summer. This is extremely common in woodland clearings and margins and constitutes an important food species for the elephant hawk moth. Towards the end of summer, if you look carefully you may notice large brown hawk moth caterpillars feeding on the plants.

Continuing, you will start to see the variety of trees (**2**) that make up Deerpark Woods. Along the stream edge ash and other broadleaves grow, and in late summer you cannot miss the rowan trees throughout the woods with their annual crop of bright red berries. The berries are an important source of food for many different birds.

Further along the trail you pass through coniferous forest. Here, Douglas fir, Sitka and Norway spruce are being grown for timber production. They also provide an important home for different wildlife – mammals such as deer find ample cover amongst the young trees, while many birds frequent the conifer woods, feeding on the profusion of seeds in the autumn.

The trail makes a sharp turn right (**3**) and leads uphill. At (**4**) continue to another viewpoint from where you can admire the scenery. Where the trail enters the forest again (**5**) you will notice the old deer park boundary wall. Keep following the blue markers and you will soon return to the car park.

The slot and droppings of roe deer (left) and red deer are not difficult to tell apart.

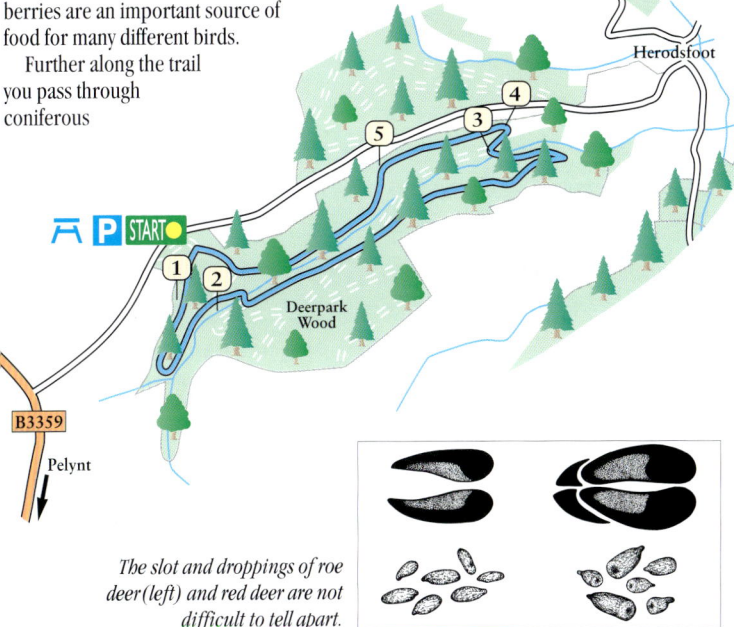

CORNWALL

Cardinham Woods

THE SILVERMINE TRAIL

Grade	▲
Distance	3½ miles (5.6km)
Timing	2 hrs
Footwear	👟
Directions	Follow blue then white waymarkers
Parking	Cardinham Woods car park – pay and display

Start point If approaching from the east, turn off the A38 at Carminnow Cross, just before the junction with the A30. At the crossroads, follow signs for Cardinham Woods. From the west, leave the A30 following signs for Bodmin. At the roundabout, take the exit for the A38. Take the first turning to the left and follow signs for Cardinham Woods. Leave the car park on the riverside walk, following the blue waymarkers.

Cardinham Wood was, until recently, leased by the Forestry Commission from Llanhydrock Estate and Glynn. Its earliest history was recorded after the Norman invasion and relates to the Priory of Tywardreath and the monks at 'La Capella de Valle in Cornubia'. In the year 1200 Robert de Cardinan granted to the monks of Tywardreath the Mill of Cardinan and whatever they might require of the woods for building and firing, and for pannage (hunting for acorns) for the priory pigs.

At (**1**), where the trail leads into the forest above the woodland café, look out for wooden bat boxes positioned in some of the trees. Two species of bat are known to have used these – pipistrelle and brown long-eared bats. Also, depending on the time of year, you may see common lizards and several species of butterfly on the forest road edge.

Follow the trail as it bears to the right (**2**) and crosses the river, at which point you will notice Lady Vale Bridge on your right. This clapper bridge takes its name from the 'Chapel of our Lady of the Vale' which stood near here from about 1170. Unfortunately you cannot see any of the remains today. Please do not climb on the old bridge.

Leave the riverside trail and follow the white waymarkers for the Silvermine Trail along the first track on your left after the river crossing. The river is Cardinham Water, which is a tributary of the Fowey, and this is a very important stretch of water as it provides a valuable habitat for trout, salmon and otters.

Keep an eye open for some of the wildlife that inhabits the forest. Red and roe deer can be found at Cardinham and buzzards can be seen soaring high over the Glynn valley.

The trail climbs up through the forest to join another forest road which leads to the remains of the Hurstocks lead and silver mine (**3**). The mine was last worked in the 19th century and now serves as a reminder of a bygone era when mining was one of Cornwall's main industries.

The small Lady Vale clapper bridge at Cardinham, close to the site of a 12th-century chapel.

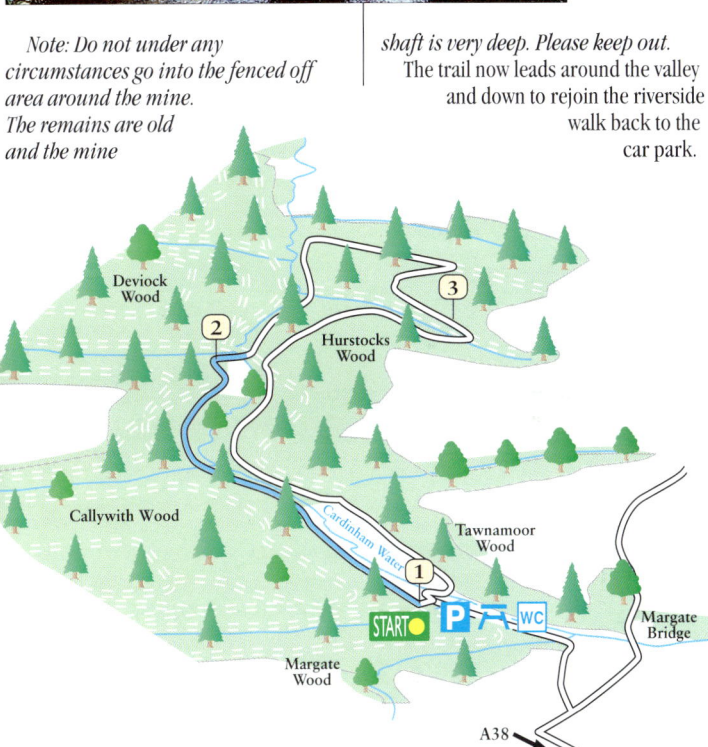

Note: Do not under any circumstances go into the fenced off area around the mine. The remains are old and the mine shaft is very deep. Please keep out. The trail now leads around the valley and down to rejoin the riverside walk back to the car park.

CORNWALL

Guide to common trees

DOUGLAS FIR
Named after David Douglas, who in 1827 sent the first seed back to Britain. It is a valuable timber tree used for sawmill timber and paper pulp.

HYBRID LARCH
The result of the chance cross-pollination of Japanese and European larch at the turn of the century. Strong, durable timber used for fencing, rails and gates.

SCOTS PINE
A native of the once extensive Caledonian Pine Forests, it is Britain's only native timber producing conifer. Used for telegraph poles, furniture and paper pulp.

WILD CHERRY
A fast growing deciduous native found in mixed and beech woods throughout Britain. Used for fine furniture, musical instruments and smoking pipes.

HAZEL
The ideal coppice tree in that every few years it can be cut back to a 'stool' at ground level so that it produces a cluster of straight flexible stems to be harvested. Traditionally used for firewood, 'wattle and daub' building and thatching spars.

WEST COUNTRY

NORWAY SPRUCE
The traditional Christmas Tree found in many homes during December. Its timber is used for internal building work and is ideal for parts of violins.

OAK
Held sacred by the Druids, pedunculate or English oak has always been important. Strong, durable timber used for furniture and barrels. The sawdust is used for smoking food.

CORSICAN PINE
This variety of Black pine is fast growing and has a remarkably straight trunk which is lightly branched. Used traditionally for railway sleepers.

ASH
Said to have mystical and medicinal properties, this is a widespread native tree whose wood is a natural shock absorber. Ideal for tool handles, oars, hockey sticks, rackets and flooring.

YEW
One of the oldest living trees in Northern Europe, yews are a primitive form of conifer, native to Britain. Although a 'softwood', it grows slowly, giving the wood great strength. Its branches were once used for making longbows; today the wood is made into veneers.

WOODLAND WALKS

Guide to common trees

SYCAMORE
Brought from France in the Middle Ages, the sycamore seeds profusely. Once popular for kitchen surfaces and utensils, now used for violins and veneers.

SWEET CHESTNUT
Introduced into Britain by the Romans, who ground up the nuts to make 'polenta', a staple food. Strong timber which is good for joinery, cabinet-making and fencing.

BEECH
Characteristic of chalk downlands but also found elsewhere on light soils. Sometimes called 'Lady of the Woods', its wood was once used for rifle butts and shoe heels.

BIRCH
Despite its graceful appearance, it is one of Britain's hardiest trees. Found throughout the country, its wood is used for plywood production, toys and reels, and its twigs are cut to make horse jumps.

ROWAN
Often called the Mountain ash, although no relation to the ash, it is found higher up mountains than any other tree. Used traditionally for longbows.

LEAF AND BARK DETAILS ARE GIVEN ON THE NEXT PAGES

The information on the following pages will tell you more about some of the trees you will encounter on these woodland walks, helping you to identify some of the most common species, particularly through leaf and bark types.

CORSICAN PINE
The fissured dark greyish-brown bark breaks off.

YEW
The light brown bark becomes deeply furrowed and breaks away in long flakes.

WILD CHERRY
Smooth, purplish-brown bark with metallic lustre and horizontal bands of lenticels.

OAK
The bark becomes fissured with age.

ASH
The bark is smooth and greenish-grey, turning grey and fissuring with age.

SYCAMORE
The smooth grey bark falls away to reveal orange-brown bark below.

SWEET CHESTNUT
The bark has long diagonal fissures.

BEECH
The bark is smooth and grey.

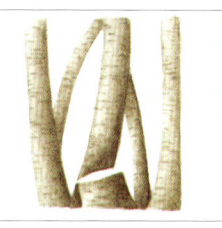

HAZEL
Smooth, shiny brown bark with conspicuous yellow lenticels and scaly patches.

WOODLAND WALKS

CORSICAN PINE
Large, shining cones, always one-sided or oblique. The needles are long and in pairs.

YEW
The seed is like most of the tree, poisonous to man but not to deer or rabbits.

WILD CHERRY
White flowers are followed by small green cherries which turn red then purple.

OAK
Most oaks do not grow acorns until over 50 years old. The female flowers are on stalks.

ASH
The distinctive black winter buds produce clusters of small purple flowers.

SYCAMORE
The winged seeds usually fall together. The leaves often have 'tar spots' caused by fungus.

SWEET CHESTNUT
Some catkins have male and female flowers on one stalk. The husk splits to release nuts.

BEECH
In the autumn, the leaves turn yellow then bronze. The husks release two triangular seeds.

HAZEL
The leaves are placed alternately along the twigs and open in late April.

WEST COUNTRY

Useful Information

For further information about the forests, woodlands and walks contained in this guide, please contact:

Forest Enterprise District Office
Bullers Hill
Kennford
Exeter
Devon
EX6 7XR
Tel. 01392 832262

Forest Enterprise District Office
Coldharbour
Wareham
Dorset
BH20 7PA
Tel. 01929 552074

Permits for horse riding should also be obtained from these offices.

Forest Enterprise provides many other opportunities for you to visit and enjoy walking in forests and woodlands throughout Britain. We have many hundreds of trails and car parks similar to the ones described in this guide, and some of our larger forests are designated as Forest Parks. Many of these have Forest Shops and Visitor Centres, which are ideal places to discover the variety of forests and facilities on offer.

We also manage a number of camping and cabin sites around Britain under the title of 'Forest Enterprise Holidays'.

Many of our forests are also accessible for other recreational activities such as cycling, horse riding, orienteering and special events. We also organise guided walks, details of which are in 'What's On', available from Visitor and Tourist Information Centres or Forest Offices.

For further information about recreational opportunities in your forests or 'Forest Enterprise Holidays', please contact us at:

Forest Enterprise
231 Corstorphine Road
Edinburgh
Scotland
EH12 7AT
Tel. 0131 334 0303

Ordnance Survey Maps

The areas incuded in this guide are covered by the following Ordnance Survey Pathfinder maps at 1:25 000 scale:

1216	1314	1348
1275	1315	1349
1278	1329	1356
1312	1347	

Outdoor Leisure Maps at 1:25 000 scale cover Britain's National Parks and Areas of Outstanding Natural Beauty. Relevant to the West Country are:

OLM 9 (Exmoor)
OLM 15 (Purbeck & South Dorset)
OLM 22 (New Forest)
OLM 28 (Dartmoor)

To find the walks in this guide, use the OS Great Britain Routeplanner Travelmaster map number 1 at 1:625 000 (1 inch to 10 miles, or 1cm to 6.25km) or Travelmaster map 8 (South West England and South Wales) and Travelmaster map 9 (South East England) at 1:250 000 (1 inch to 4 miles, or 1 cm to 2.5km).

WOODLAND WALKS

Index

Abbeyford Wood 38
Alder 49
Affpuddle Forest 24
Area of Outstanding
    Natural Beauty 13
Ash 59, 61, 62
Ashclyst Forest 30
Ashton 40
Assycombe Brook 49

Beech 27, 42, 44, 46,
    60, 61, 62
Bellever Forest 46
Bellever Tor 46
Birch 20, 23, 27, 39
    Silver 22
Bird of Prey Viewpoint
    41
Blackdown Hills 26
Borington Camp 53
Bramble Brook 44, 45
Bristol Channel 26
Broadclyst 31
Brookes Ride 44
Buckland Abbey Estate
    50
Bullers Hill 40, 41, 45

Canonteign Forest 45
Cann Wood 52
Cardinham Woods 56
Castle Neroche Forest
    Trail 26
Chaldon Down 24
Cherry 42
    Wild 58, 61, 62
Clapper bridges 46
Coppicing 32
Cullpepper's Dish 24
Dartmoor 41, 44
Dawlish Warren Nature
    Reserve 43
Deadman's Combe 41
Deerpark Woods 54
Denham Forest 50

Douglas Fir 28, 33, 35,
    36, 39, 46, 49, 55, 58
Duchy of Cornwall 48

Eggesford Wood 34
Exeter 41
Exmouth 43

Fauna 13
Fernworthy Forest 48
Forest Code 15
Forestry Commission
    10
France Brook 40

Glastonbury Tor 26

Haldon Forest 40, 42,
    44
    Hills 31, 43
    Ridge 13, 40
Hangman's Grit 29
Hawthorn 23
Haytor 41, 45, 46
Hazel 32, 34, 53, 58,
    61, 62
Hennock 40, 45
Herodsfoot valley 54
History 9
Hurn Forest 19, 20

Isle of Wight 21

Lady Vale Bridge 56
Lakehead Hill 46
Lakehead Newtake 46
Larch 28, 33, 39, 46
    Hybrid 58
    Japanese 53
Lawrence Tower 40
Lawrence, General
    Stringer 40
Lawson Cypresses 33
Lee Moor 53
Llanhydrock 56
Lord's Ball 29
Lowton Brook 49
Lucy Ball Plantation 40

Lydford 47
Lympstone 43

Mamhead 42
Monkey Puzzle 37
Moors Valley Forest 18
Morden Bog 22
Moreton Forest 24
Mountain Ash 48

Neroche 26
Nether Stowey 28

Oak 20, 23, 27, 28, 29,
    42, 51, 59, 61, 62
Oakers Wood 25

Pallington Forest 24
Pine
    Corsican 19, 22, 23,
        24, 31, 43, 59, 61, 62
    Lodgepole 22
    Maritime 21, 22
    Monterey 23
    Scots 19, 21, 22, 23,
        42, 58
Poole Pasin 19
Powerline Butterfly
    Meadows 30
Powerline Forest Nature
    Reserve 45
Priory of Tywardreath
    56
Purbeck Hills 19, 24

Quantock
    Combe 29
    Forest 28
    Hills 26

Rams Combe 29
Ramsdown Forest
    Nature Reserve 20
Rimsmoor Pond 25
Ringwood Forest 18
River Exe 32, 33

River Stour 21
Rowan 48, 60

Saltram Estate 52
Sedgemoor 26
Seven Wells 29
Shaugh Prior 53
Sika Trail 22
Silver Jubilee 45
Site of Special Scientific
    Interest 13
Springetts Wood 39
Spruce
    Norway 55, 59
    Sitka 19, 28, 31, 41,
        43, 45, 46
Stoke
    Hill 32
    Woods 32
Sweet Chestnut 42, 53,
    60, 61, 62
Sycamore 32, 44, 60,
    61, 62

Tarka Project 37
Tavy valley 50
Taw valley 34
Teign valley 41
Thornworthy Tor 49
Tims Bridge 49
Tower Park 19
Tower Wood 41

Vale of Taunton 26

Wareham Forest 22
West Hill 29
Williamson, Henry 37,
    39
Willow 23
Winfrith 24
World War II 21, 45
Wych Elm 32

Yew 59, 61, 62

WOODLAND WALKS